D1568608

Stars
of the Ziegfeld Follies

Showgirls in a scene from the first Ziegfeld Follies, which opened in New York City in 1907. Florenz Ziegfeld produced a new Follies show every season for 20 years, from 1907 to 1927.

A Pull Ahead Book

STARS OF THE ZIEGFELD FOLLIES

Julien Phillips

Lerner Publications Company • Minneapolis, Minnesota

ACKNOWLEDGMENTS: The illustrations are reproduced through the courtesy of: pp. 2, 9, Independent Picture Service; pp. 5, 6, 10, 11, 13, 15, 16, 24, 28, 36, 49, 58, 63, 66, 74, 77, Theatre Collection, The New York Public Library, Astor, Lenox and Tilden Foundations; pp. 12, 19, 21, 27, 31, 34, 41, 45, 46, 54, 57, Picture Collection, The New York Public Library; pp. 22, 32, 39, 42, 61, 65, 71, United Press International; p. 50, Cherokee Book Shop; p. 53, Underwood & Underwood; p. 69, Will Rogers Memorial, Claremore, Oklahoma.

LIBRARY OF CONGRESS CATALOGING IN PUBLICATION DATA

Phillips, Julien.
    Stars of the Ziegfeld Follies.

    (A Pull Ahead Book)
    SUMMARY: A brief biography of Ziegfeld, creator of the famous musical reviews, and profiles of some of the performers who starred in his productions.

    1. Ziegfeld, Florenz, 1869-1932—Juvenile literature. 2. Actors, American—Biography—Juvenile literature.   [1. Ziegfeld, Florenz, 1869-1932. 2. Actors] I. Title.

PN2287.Z5P5   790.2'0922 [B] [920]   72-165324
ISBN   0-8225-0464-2

International Standard Book Number: 0-8225-0464-2
Library of Congress Catalog Card Number: 72-165324

Second Printing 1973

contents

Showgirl wearing a peacock costume in the Follies of 1925.

Cobra costume worn by showgirl Imogene Wilson in a 1920s Follies. Fantastic and luxurious costumes were important features of every Ziegfeld Follies.

The Ziegfeld Follies

During almost 20 years near the beginning of this century, "The Ziegfeld Follies" was a magical name to people all over the United States. When people thought of the Follies they thought of the most beautiful girls in the world. They thought of the funniest comedians and the most lavish costumes and sets. And they thought of the newest music, songs, and dances. Every girl who dreamed of becoming a star dreamed of being chosen by Florenz Ziegfeld for his Follies. Everyone who was anyone would be in the audience on opening night in New York City. The Follies were not just the finest entertainment in New York. They were masterpieces of color and beauty and sound.

Yet the Follies started modestly enough with a very small ad. Ziegfeld had it printed at the bottom of a weekly vaudeville bill for a theatre called the Jardin de Paris. Nearly a month later a bigger ad appeared. It announced that the Jardin de Paris was a refreshing place to get away from the city. Actually, the Jardin de Paris was a small, hot, and stuffy roof garden that had a stage. The roof leaked when it rained. But on July 9, 1907, people came there to see the first Ziegfeld Follies. They liked the show they saw. It was exciting and different. The next morning one newspaper said: "Mr. Florenz Ziegfeld has given New York quite the best melange of mirth, music, and pretty young women that has been seen here in many summers. There is not a dull moment in the entire show." Ziegfeld and his Follies were on their way.

Chorus line in the Follies of 1907. The first Follies was very successful, in part because Ziegfeld was a master at making pretty girls look even prettier.

Theatres usually closed during the summer, but Ziegfeld played the Follies throughout July, August, and September. In the fall he moved the Follies to the Liberty Theatre in New York. And still the people kept coming to see his show. Yet no one at the time, including Ziegfeld, expected that the Follies would last for 21 years. Critics said they were a fad that would end as quickly as it began.

A lavish scene from the Follies of 1919, which was considered one of Ziegfeld's greatest shows.

The Follies did change a lot as the years passed, but they didn't disappear. They attracted more and more star performers. They became more lavish. They became more expensive to stage and to run. For example, the average salary of performers in the early years was $75 a week. By 1921 performers like Will Rogers and Fanny Brice were making between $2,000 and $3,000 a week. And as the Follies became more expensive to stage and operate, they also became more expensive to see. People paid $16 for one ticket. Opening night tickets went for as much as $75 each. At those prices, a Follies show was not just an evening's entertainment. It was an event.

Lillian Lorraine, one of Ziegfeld's most beautiful girls, appeared in the Follies from 1910 through 1918.

Many people have said that the greatest period of the Follies was from 1914 to 1921. Old-timers of the theatre insist that the shows of 1918 and 1919 were real theatrical masterpieces. The list of performers for those two years included Marilyn Miller, Bert Williams, Will Rogers, dancer Ann Pennington, Eddie Cantor, the great beauty Lillian Lorraine, W. C. Fields, and Fanny Brice. Most producers would have been content with one of these stars for his show. Ziegfeld wanted them all.

Ruth Etting was a Follies girl in 1927 and 1931, and a star of the Ziegfeld musical *Whoopee* from 1928 to 1930.

Jessica Reed, one of Ziegfeld's highest paid showgirls, first appeared in the Follies of 1920.

What made the Ziegfeld Follies so popular? They seemed to have a magic combination of ingredients—singers, costumes, dancers, sets, and comedians. But certainly much of the Follies' success depended on Ziegfeld. He had an excellent sense for color and lighting and effective staging of visual spectacles. He also had excellent judgement about female beauty and a talent for "glorifying" beautiful women.

A Ziegfeld girl had only to walk across the stage or appear in a richly decorated scene and every man in the audience would fall in love with her. Or so the legend goes. In 1922 the Follies were officially subtitled "Glorifying the American Girl." For his taste and skill, Ziegfeld had earlier earned the name The Great Glorifier. But perhaps Ziegfeld's first wife described him just as well when she said: "Ziegfeld is a very, very good manager."

Mae Murray was a Follies dancer early in the 1920s and later became a Hollywood star.

Florenz Ziegfeld as a young man.

Florenz Ziegfeld
(1869-1932)

The man who created all the beauty and success of the Follies was Florenz Ziegfeld. Ziegfeld was born in Chicago in 1868. His father was a dedicated musician and hoped that his son Florenz would grow up to be a musician. But Ziegfeld had little interest in studying or practicing music. In fact he seemed to have little interest in anything until his parents sent him to a cattle ranch in Wyoming while he was still a teen-ager. It seems that he came back from the ranch full of health and energy. There are stories that he also came back with enough independence to join Buffalo Bill and his Wild West Show when they came through Chicago. His father caught up with him and took him home. But Ziegfeld, as the story goes, had had his first taste of show business.

In 1892 Ziegfeld's father sent him to Europe to round up musical entertainment for a show at the Chicago World's Fair. Ziegfeld came back with several European musical groups, including the highly admired Hans von Bulow orchestra. But Chicago Fair-goers were not interested, and the concerts rapidly began to lose money. Again Ziegfeld went searching for talent. In New York he found the strong man Eugene Sandow. When Sandow replaced the orchestra on stage, the show became popular and successful. And Ziegfeld began in earnest his career as a promoter and producer.

After a few years of touring with Sandow, Ziegfeld went to Europe. There he found Anna Held. Anna sang in music hall revues. She was short, mischievous, pretty, and just a little bit naughty. She teased and sang "Won't You Come and Play Wiz Me?" At once Ziegfeld thought he could make her a star. He offered her an unheard-of $1,000 a week to come to America. She accepted. Ziegfeld did not immediately star her in a show. At first she sang a program of songs between the acts of a musical play he had revived. Ziegfeld knew what he was doing. He wanted the public to feel they had "discovered" Anna. They did; she was an instant success. Then, with starring roles and more publicity, Anna Held became very famous. In 1897 she also became Mrs. Florenz Ziegfeld.

Anna Held gave Ziegfeld the idea for the Follies. In France the Folies Bergere was immensely popular. It was a variety show with singing and dancing and beautiful girls. Anna told Ziegfeld about the Folies and also told him that American girls were just as pretty as French girls. "Flo" listened to what she said and decided to produce an American follies. His follies would have many beautiful girls who had grace and elegance. It would have lavish costumes and sets, the finest musicians, and the best comedians. And it would be successful.

Anna Held, Ziegfeld's first wife. She gave Ziegfeld the idea to do an American Follies like the Folies Bergere in Paris.

The first Ziegfeld Follies, with singers, a burlesque team, comedians, and other performers, opened in New York on July 9, 1907. The main attraction was a chorus of 50 girls called The Anna Held Girls. (Anna Held herself never appeared in the Follies.) The whole show, which had cost $13,000 to stage, was an overnight success.

During the next 20 years, Ziegfeld spent a lot of money on the costumes and sets for his Follies. (One of the last Follies cost $200,000 to produce and about $30,000 a week to run.) And the money he spent helped to make the shows the successes they were. He knew that Miss Held's costumes had always attracted attention. She was famous for her sable coats, jeweled shoes, lace corsets, and pearls, diamonds, rubies, and sapphires. Her stage costumes were talked about by everyone. One famous dress, The Poppy Dress, cost about $20,000. It was trimmed with all shades of poppies in full bloom. People came to her show just to see this fantastic dress.

The Dolly Sisters, a famous pair of twins who appeared in the Follies. Ziegfeld loved to see The Sisters, and all the Follies girls, dressed in rich, extravagant costumes on stage.

So Ziegfeld bought the finest materials for the Follies girls. Flo's expensive-looking shows were expensive. He often used furs, real flowers, jewels, and real laces. He made sure that all the ribbons, linings, and trimmings were of the best possible quality. When he saw finished costumes, the first thing he did was turn them inside out to make sure the linings were of as good quality as the rest of the costumes. He believed the girls walked and acted more gracefully if the linings made them feel elegant.

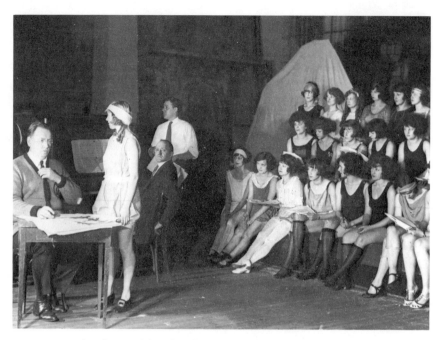

A rehearsal for the dancers in the Follies of 1923.

In addition to producing the Follies, in 1914 Ziegfeld opened a nightclub called the Midnight Frolic. The show at the Frolic was smaller than the Follies, but just as lavish. Many performers who became top stars—for instance, Will Rogers and Eddie Cantor—were first hired by Ziegfeld for the Frolic. If they were successful, they were moved on to the Follies. The Frolic was closed in 1921, but by then Ziegfeld was doing musical shows, such as *Showboat*, as well as the Follies. Florenz Ziegfeld was at the top of the entertainment world.

And he lived up to his position with whatever money could buy. Ziegfeld had always been known as a man who spent great amounts of money, whether he had it or not. Flo had never seemed to care how much things cost or whether he should save for a rainy day. He just bought whatever caught his fancy and worried about paying for it later—if at all. When he was courting Billie Burke, who later became his second wife, he sent her so many flowers that her dressing room looked like a greenhouse. (Flo never sent someone a simple bouquet when he could send vases and vases of flowers.) Later, Miss Burke told him she had tried to call and thank him but his phone had been busy. He immediately had a special phone installed just for her use.

Billie Burke, Ziegfeld's second wife, was a well-known stage and screen actress.

Florenz Ziegfeld was in many ways a strange man. Instead of using a suitcase when he traveled, "Ziggy" carried his clothes and toothbrush rolled up in a newspaper. He enjoyed practical jokes but rarely laughed at the antics of his star comedians. He was superstitious about his shows and made sure there was an animal—elephant, cat, horse, chimpanzee—in every one for good luck. One of his favorite means of communication was the telegram. If Flo wanted to talk to someone on stage, often he didn't talk to him over the footlights or even wait until he got off stage. Ziggy would race to his office and send him a telegram. These telegrams were sometimes five pages or more long and included a note saying "details will follow later."

By the mid-1920s many of Ziegfeld's big stars began leaving the Follies—Fanny Brice in 1923, Will Rogers in 1924, W. C. Fields in 1925, and Eddie Cantor in 1927. But the Follies were still a national institution. It took the stockmarket crash of 1929 to bring an end to the height of Flo Ziegfeld's career. He was still ordering private railroad cars and sending flowers and telegrams lavishly, but it was all a sham. Ziegfeld had lost millions. In addition, he was ill. Some of his friends maintained that the loss of his fortune and his position in the entertainment world helped to push him to his grave. The Great Glorifier died in 1932, and was buried in a simple ceremony in Los Angeles, California.

Florenz Ziegfeld in 1932, shortly before his death.

Eugene Sandow

Eugene Sandow

(1867-1925)

Eugene Sandow was the strong man who boosted Florenz Ziegfeld's show business career into the big time. When the orchestras Ziegfeld had engaged for the Chicago World's Fair of 1892 proved unpopular, he went to New York to find other entertainers. He found Sandow, a muscle man from England, performing an intermission act at the Casino Theatre. Sandow had not been doing very well in New York. But when Ziegfeld heard some of the ladies in the audience squeal during Sandow's act, he decided he wanted the strong man in Chicago. At first Sandow refused to come unless Ziegfeld paid him $1,000 a week—a tremendous amount of money for an entertainer in those days. But Ziegfeld, who was nearly broke at the time, made a deal that instead Sandow would get 10 per cent of the receipts. (That 10 per cent soon amounted to $3,000 a week.)

With Sandow in tow, Ziegfeld spent his last $5,000 on an all-out advertising campaign, billing him as the strongest man in the world, The Great Sandow. Then Ziegfeld insured his success by selling special tickets to Chicago's society women. These tickets allowed them to go backstage after the show and feel Sandow's muscles. After Mrs. Potter Palmer, a leading society matron, had felt The Great Sandow's amazing muscles, it became the thing to do. Everyone who was anyone went to see the strong man. And those who had special tickets got an added thrill after the show.

After the World's Fair was over, Ziegfeld toured the country with Sandow for more than three years. During that time Ziegfeld publicized quite a few fantastic feats of strength that he claimed The Great Sandow had accomplished. Actually, Ziegfeld had them "arranged." For example, once while their train was delayed, Ziegfeld spotted an iron wheel from a wrecked train. He paid about 20 men to carry it to Sandow's compartment. When they arrived in California, Ziegfeld interviewed reporters in Sandow's compartment, where he casually pointed to the huge iron wheel and told the reporters that Sandow had brought it along as a souvenir.

When Ziegfeld and The Great Sandow went to San Francisco, people there showed little interest in the strong man. So Ziegfeld stirred up some excitement. A lion had just escaped from a local amusement park and had eaten a keeper. This gave Ziegfeld an idea. He arranged for a match between Sandow and "Wallace, The Man-Eating Lion." As they were supposed to, many people confused Wallace with the escaped lion, and a huge audience went to see the Sandow-Wallace fight.

A stage was set up and separated from the audience by iron bars. When Sandow reached over and patted Wallace on his whiskers, Wallace leaped from his pen and roared. The audience bubbled with excitement. Wallace was excited

The Great Sandow at the height of his career as "the strongest man in the world."

too. He was an old, peaceful lion, but he had just received an electric shock through the floor of his pen. As he came down through the air, The Great Sandow hit him. But Wallace didn't want to fight. He crept away from Sandow and cowered in a corner. The crowd was furious. This was no man-eating lion. It was an old, frightened lion, and they wanted their money back. But it was no use. Ziegfeld had already left town with the receipts.

Anna Held, in costume for a Ziegfeld production, the play *La Poupée* (*The Doll*).

Anna Held

(1873-1918)

Anna Held was 22 years old when Ziegfeld found her in London in 1896. The story goes that her father was a French glovemaker who had died while she was very young. Anna and her mother worked in Paris until they saved some money. Then they went to London. There Anna got her first job in the theatre, as a chorus girl, when she was only 12 years old. With experience and some training, she went on to become a solo performer.

When Ziegfeld first saw her she was already a popular entertainer. Ziegfeld was impressed. Anna was charming and flirtatious and attractive. She was very short and curvaceous. (She laced in her waist to a tiny 18 inches.) But most of all she had something "special" on stage.

When Anna first came to America, Ziegfeld arranged a press conference for her. She talked about bloomers, about bicycling, and about London and how much she loved it. She laughed and smiled and flirted. She wore the latest style of clothing. (Later she was to start the newest fads.) She was full of fun and femininity and the American public loved her immediately.

Anna Held wearing a stylish Parisian fashion. Women all over America wanted to know and copy what Anna was wearing.

Her publicity was often more dramatic than her stage performance. When automobile racing became a fad in America, Miss Held said that women should take it up. She announced that she would be glad to race from New York to Philadelphia against any woman driving a car. Miss Held added that she had driven a lot in France. In fact, she said she held some speed records for driving. A race never took place, but the publicity had already served its purpose.

Another time Ziegfeld arranged for Anna to take part in a kissing contest. A young man had bet that he could kiss Anna 200 times without losing his enthusiasm. He lost his bet, but Anna gained lots of attention in the newspapers.

But perhaps the best publicity Anna ever got was over milk baths. Ziegfeld began ordering many gallons of milk each day. It seemed impossible that anyone could drink so much milk. Then a newspaper reporter who investigated was told that Anna bathed in milk. She said that she kept her body beautiful and her complexion silky with daily milk baths. When the publicity began to die down, Ziegfeld brought back public attention. He had the milkman sue him for refusing to pay for the milk. Ziegfeld defended himself by saying that the milk was sour and was ruining Miss Held's complexion. Women all over America began bathing in milk — and feeling sticky.

Beneath the surface, however, Anna Held's life was not all glamour. She had been married and divorced before she came to the United States. She had one daughter from her former marriage. After she married him, Ziegfeld spent much of his time during the early years of the 1900s gambling and wasting fantastic sums of money in Europe. Anna complained that she and her daughter were neglected. In 1913 Anna and Ziegfeld were divorced; a year later he married Billie Burke. Anna Held's early death in 1918 was not particularly glamorous.

Bert Williams

Bert Williams

(1876-1922)

In 1876 Egbert Austin Williams was born in the West Indies, where his grandfather had been a Danish consul and his grandmother a beauty of Spanish and African descent. A series of misfortunes struck his family while "Bert" was quite young. First, his family lost their money. Then, his father's health began to fail and he was advised to leave the islands. So the family moved to San Pedro, California. But despite the misfortunes, Bert was a happy child. And even as a small boy in California, he showed a talent for singing and for imitating nearly everything. His "talent" was sometimes exasperating to his parents, but in time it would lead him to become one of the greatest comedians of his day.

After finishing high school, Bert studied civil engineering for a while. But then he decided to try a career in show business. He joined a group of three other boys and toured California with them. They played Hawaiian music from town to town. During this time Bert was growing more and more interested in becoming a minstrel. The minstrel show was a very popular form of entertainment near the turn of the century. It was also one of the few areas of show business open to Negro performers. A typical minstrel show consisted of a group of performers who sang Negro melodies, played banjos, told jokes, and did impersonations. Minstrels, white or black, blackened their faces with burnt cork and spoke in Negro dialect on the stage. When Bert Williams made up his mind to become a minstrel, he discovered he first had to learn the American Negro dialect. He also had to learn the kind of slapstick humor audiences of his time required of a black man. However, Bert was a careful listener and observer. And he had a great talent for imitation and a natural sense of humor. Williams was destined to delight audiences all over Europe and America.

In 1895 he formed a vaudeville team with George Walker. Together they began to break away from some of the limitations of the minstrel show. In 1902 the pair starred in the first all-Negro comedy to capture Broadway's attention. The show, *In Dahomey*, was immensely successful—so successful that Williams and Walker took it to England. It was also important. *In Dahomey* represented a major effort by black performers to gain recognition in the theatre. They hoped to shake off the invisible chains that kept them from doing serious drama. The comedy team of Williams and Walker continued to do shows together until Walker's death in 1909.

Bert Williams was a tall, handsome, gifted performer. But because he was a Negro, Williams never got a chance to do serious drama.

Then for 10 years Williams worked as a star comedian in Florenz Ziegfeld's fabulous Follies. Bert won great fame with Ziegfeld. He had an excellent sense of timing, and he was a master of pantomime. Audiences were delighted by his comedy routines, which seemed so simple and natural.

But Williams had worked hard to make them "natural." (He had even studied pantomime in Europe with Pietro, the greatest pantomimist of the time.) He used pauses after gestures because they made the gestures more meaningful. He used simple actions because they were more effective than complicated ones. He observed the behavior of people carefully and used actions from real life on the stage. Bert Williams never "hammed it up" to draw laughter. Comedians who learned from Williams, such as Eddie Cantor and W. C. Fields, said that Bert never moved his hand six inches if three inches would do.

Most of Williams' comic material sprang from the idea that he was getting the worst of a situation. He himself described his kind of humor by saying that if it were raining soup, he would have a fork in his hand instead of a spoon. In his shows with Walker, Bert had portrayed a kindly, rather simple, hard-luck type. His flashy, dishonest partner was always taking advantage of him.

Much of Williams' hard-luck humor was based on his own experiences of being a black man. Even at the height of his career with the Ziegfeld Follies, Williams was allowed to live in a good New York City hotel only provided he use the back elevator. And his lifelong desire to perform in serious drama was only an impossible dream because of the

Bert Williams in the blackface he wore for his comedy acts.

racial barriers at that time. W. C. Fields, who was a close friend of Williams, described him as "the funniest man I ever saw and the saddest man I ever knew." However, only Bert's close friends ever saw his sorrow. Bert Williams did not wear bitterness on his sleeve.

But, like Fanny Brice, one of this great comedian's greatest triumphs with the usually fun-loving Ziegfeld audience came from a sad song. Like Fanny Brice singing "My Man," Bert Williams sang "Nobody" straight from his heart: "I ain't never done nothin' to nobody/ I ain't never got nothin' from nobody no time."

Fanny Brice in 1920.

Fanny Brice
(1891-1951)

Fanny Brice was born on the Lower East Side of New York City. Her real name was Fanny Borach. Fanny loved to perform from the time she was a little girl. With a gang of kids, she sang in backyards for pennies. She sang for her family, standing on top of her father's bar. (Her parents owned a saloon, where they sold beer for a nickel a glass and served free lunches.)

When Fanny Borach was 13 she made her first stage appearance at Keeney's Theatre in Brooklyn on amateur night. She and her brother went to the theatre to see the show. But they had only two quarters, and the quarter seats were sold out. So they went backstage, and Fanny told the manager that she wanted to perform. He let them in. They planned to sneak out a little while before Fanny's turn on stage came. But she was caught off guard and actually pushed onto the stage. Fanny Borach was terrified, but the audience encouraged her to sing "When You Know You're Not Forgotten by the Girl You Can't Forget." She won the first prize of five dollars. (Fanny claimed she won only because she had so many friends in the audience.) Her career had begun.

•

After that, Fanny did almost everything she could to get her stage name, Fanny Brice, in lights. That wasn't easy for a skinny girl who wasn't pretty and couldn't dance. But Fanny could sing, and she was determined. Finally, a burlesque manager hired her. He heard her sing and put her in a chorus, supposing she could dance. After a few rehearsals, Fanny was moved to the back of the stage in the last row of the chorus. But Fanny gave away her underwear to the other chorus girls in return for dancing lessons. And on her own she understudied the show's lead singer.

One night the lead singer fainted; she couldn't go on. Fanny was told to go on in her place. The lead singer was rather fat and lumpy, but she had a sweet, melodic voice and she knew how to dance gracefully. Fanny knew she couldn't compete by trying to sing the song as the other woman had. Instead, Fanny sang quickly and spiritedly. She exaggerated the few dance steps she knew. She was full of life, and the audience caught her spirit and sense of fun. So did the owner of the burlesque hall, who watched the show from the audience that night. He liked Fanny so much that she did the song from that time on. The other singer went back to the chorus.

Fanny Brice in an exotic costume. Fanny was no showgirl, but she could captivate an audience with her liveliness and humor.

In 1910 Ziegfeld saw Fanny Brice playing in a burlesque hall. When he sent her a message that he wanted to see her, Fanny thought it was a joke. She couldn't believe it was true until Ziegfeld had given her a contract for $75 a week. Fanny showed her copy of the contract to everyone. She showed it to her family, to her neighbors, to strangers on the street. The contract wore out. So Fanny went back to Ziegfeld for another copy, then another, and another. Finally, Ziegfeld refused to give her any more. Fanny was in nearly every one of the Follies from 1910 to 1924, but she never again had a written contract with Ziegfeld.

Fanny Brice clowns with another comedian. Her ability to twist her face into the most absurd expressions helped to make Fanny one of the top comics of her time.

Fanny was not only a good singer; she was also a first-rate comedienne. She was particularly good at making fun of people who were usually taken seriously—ballet dancers, preachers, duchesses. For example, in one Follies' skit Fanny dressed up like the silent movies star Theda Bara. (Theda was one of the 1920s' most daring sex symbols.) Fanny's skinny legs, funny facial expressions, and crazy antics made the screen star's seductive behavior look ridiculous. The audience howled with laughter at Fanny's exaggerated imitation.

However, one of Fanny Brice's greatest successes came from a serious song. In 1921 Ziegfeld gave her a French song called "Mon Homme" or "My Man." He told her to make the audience cry: the song was about a girl who had lost the man she loved. Dressed in a torn skirt with her hair and makeup mussed, Fanny sang the song with so much feeling and power that "My Man" became one of the most popular lover's laments of the era.

That song might have been written just for Fanny. In 1918 she had married Nick Arnstein, a handsome heel whom Fanny adored. A year after their marriage Arnstein was convicted for stealing $5 million in bonds and sent to Leavenworth Federal Penitentiary to serve a two-year sentence. Fanny was loyal and refused to believe Nick was guilty. But after Arnstein was released from prison, he broke her heart so many times that finally Fanny was forced to divorce him in 1927. Although she later made a "comfortable" marriage, Fanny always maintained that Nick Arnstein was the only man in her life.

Fanny Brice as one of her best known characters—"Baby Snooks," a comic spoiled brat.

After her last appearance with Ziegfeld in 1923, Fanny used her comic talent for movies and radio. One character she created—a spoiled brat called "Baby Snooks"—delighted generations of radio listeners. Fanny Brice became a very rich woman, but her life was not all laughs and smiles.

W. C. Fields

W. C. Fields
(1879-1946)

Wilbur Claude Dukenfield, W. C. Fields, ran away from home at the age of 11. He could no longer stand the severe beatings his father gave him. Fields endured great hardships to avoid going home. He slept in the open and stole what food he could get. The life of one of this century's greatest comedians began with a lot of misery and very little humor.

W. C. Fields could easily have become a bum. But Fields had ambition. He had wanted to become a juggler ever since he had seen one perform in his hometown, Philadelphia. Bill had no teacher. But he worked hard—sometimes 18 hours a day—teaching himself to do tricks. For a long time he practiced with apples. Finally, he managed to get some steel balls. When he was 14 he got his first job juggling—at an amusement park for $5 a week. Better days came with a $10-a-week job in Atlantic City. But Fields had become an excellent juggler. Before long he was touring Europe, Africa, and Australia, as well as the United States, with his juggling act.

By 1905 Fields had branched out from juggling to comic pantomime to a major speaking role in a musical show called *The Ham Tree*. W. C. Fields was clearly headed for success in show business. In 1916 Ziegfeld signed Fields for the Follies. Bill worked with the Follies for 10 years. During those years W. C. Field's big nose, top hat, and rasping, nasal voice became familiar to a generation of theatre-goers. When he started with Ziegfeld, Fields was a well-known entertainer and comedian. By the time he left the Follies for Hollywood in 1925, he was one of the top comedians in the country. For the next 20 years, until his death in 1946, Bill Fields was making one successful motion picture comedy after another.

W. C. Fields poses in one of his comedy routines.

Yet many people did not like Fields. They thought he was self-centered, temperamental, and rude. But then he had had to learn to be tough. When Bill was very young he had no one to rely upon but himself. People who knew Fields well, like Eddie Cantor and Will Rogers, had quite a different opinion of his character. Cantor described him as a true friend who had a "wonderful warmth."

There is no question, however, that Fields had many strange characteristics. For example, when he died, great amounts of money were found stashed in hundreds of banks all over the country. The money was registered under many different false names. But it had all belonged to Bill Fields. Some people thought this showed what a miser Fields was. But actually it would be more correct to say that Fields was terrified of poverty. When he became successful, he opened a bank account in every city he visited. In case he ever returned to a place, he didn't want to be stranded without money. Fields had been stranded without money too many times in his youth.

Bill Fields with three of the "props" for which he became famous—big nose, top hat, and cigar.

Another unusual thing about W. C. Fields was his knowledge. In addition to becoming a self-taught juggler, Fields also became a self-educated man. People who knew him said Bill was very well read, up on everything. Eddie Cantor, who was one of Fields "pupils," once asked him how he had learned so much with no formal education. Field's honest answer had all the trademarks of a line from one of his comic bits.

"Simple," he drawled, "simple, my boy. Started making some money and bought this trunk. Drove up to a bookstore with the trunk on the truck, carted the trunk into the store, and told the clerk to fill it up. 'With what?' the clerk asked. 'With whatever a fellow like me should read.' Two hours later I was on my way with a trunk full of knowledge."

But his success and his knowledge did not save Fields from a weakness that has ruined many men—alcohol. By the time Bill first appeared in the Follies, he was more than a heavy drinker. He was an alcoholic. His friends claimed that Fields never behaved like a drunk. But they worried that he was slowly killing himself with vast amounts of drink. And the more successful he became, the more he drank. One friend explained Bill's drinking by saying that he was essentially a shy man, a man lacking confidence. Even when his doctor told him a few years before his death that drinking was killing him, Fields did not stop. But on his death bed he whispered, "I wonder how far I might have gone if I had laid off the bottle."

W. C. Fields with comedienne Ray Dooley in the Follies of 1925.

Whatever Field's faults or virtues as a human being, it is clear today that he did go a long way in show business. Many of his films are considered classics of comedy. They are still being shown on television and in movie houses all over the country.

58

Marilyn Miller

Marilyn Miller

(1899-1936)

Marilyn Miller was one of Ziegfeld's most beautiful and talented stars. For 12 years she worked for The Great Glorifier in one successful show after another. And even before she joined the Follies in 1918, Marilyn had had a long career in show business.

When Marilyn (born Mary Ellen Reynolds) was still an infant, her mother divorced Marilyn's father. Then she joined a theatrical company and later married its leading man, Oscar Miller. Mary Ellen Reynolds became Marilyn Miller.

Marilyn made her first appearance on stage when she was four years old. Dressed in a ballet dress, Marilyn was introduced as Mademoiselle Sugarplum. She walked on tip-toe across the stage and smiled for the audience. She was an instant hit. From then on Marilyn performed with her mother, father, and two older sisters in an act called The Five Columbians.

The Miller family often had a hard time convincing the authorities in various cities that Marilyn should be allowed to perform. A child who sang and danced on the stage was not always welcome. Some people thought permitting children to entertain was immoral. But much of the success of the act depended on Marilyn's dancing. So the Millers went wherever they were allowed to perform. When they were not allowed to work in the United States they went to London. When they were not allowed to work in London they went to Scotland. Then they toured Europe.

Marilyn Miller at a rehearsal for Ziegfeld's musical *Rosalie*—
1927. Composer George Gershwin is at the piano; Florenz
Ziegfeld is on the right.

Finally, the family won a contract to play at London's
most exclusive private club. Marilyn was greatly admired.
Shortly after that she won a contract to play at the Winter
Garden in New York City. Marilyn was just 15 years old
and already appearing on Broadway. She worked at the
Winter Garden for three years. Then she worked in a show
called *Fancy Free*. And by that time Ziegfeld knew that he
wanted her for the Follies. For two years Marilyn was a
sensation in the Follies. Then she left the show to star in a
musical Ziegfeld was producing.

The show was *Sally*, and it was one of Marilyn Miller's greatest triumphs. She won great fame for her dancing and singing. Audiences were especially fond of her song "Look for the Silver Lining." People knew that Marilyn herself had had more than her share of tragedy. So when she sang of finding happiness in the middle of unhappiness, people in the audience believed they could find happiness too.

Marilyn had married a man named Frank Carter in 1920. They had met each other at the Winter Garden. They were both talented performers, and they adored each other. But Carter was killed in an automobile accident about a year after they were married. Marilyn was a widow at the age of 21.

Marilyn Miller in Ziegfeld's musical *Sally*—1920.

But Marilyn was also a star. She seemed to have everything to live for. Yet her life became more and more unhappy. After Frank Carter died, Marilyn began to lose herself in parties, drinking, and handsome men. She married Jack Pickford in 1922 and divorced him in 1927. She was nearly the cause of a divorce between Ziegfeld and his second wife, Billie Burke. But Miss Burke was convinced that Ziegfeld was not in love with Marilyn. So she ignored the scandal that Marilyn had started. By 1930 Marilyn's personal life was a complete shambles.

Miss Miller—1922.

Yet during all this time, Miss Miller was starring in one theatrical success after another. Ziegfeld was paying her $5,000 a week. And not until 1930 did he begin to lose his enchantment with her as an actress. But then Marilyn's career began to slip. She missed important rehearsals for Ziegfeld's new musical, *Smiles*. Because of that the show was not as successful as it should have been.

Four years later the lovely Marilyn Miller died at the age of 37 from complications following a minor operation.

Will Rogers is acting a bit bashful with one of the beautiful Follies girls.

Will Rogers

(1879-1935)

Will Rogers was born in 1879 in Oolagah, Indian Territory, which was to become part of the state of Oklahoma. By the time he was 14 years old, Will was working as a cowhand. He had attended school because his mother wanted him to become a minister. But Will didn't like school. He wanted to see the world, not study.

Rogers had heard that Argentina was a wonderful place for cowboys. So in 1902 he shipped out of New York for Buenos Aires with a friend. Unfortunately, when they got there, Will found out that the Argentines had no need for American cowboys. His friend gave up and went home, but Rogers decided to stick it out for a while.

Next Will headed for South Africa, working his way across the Atlantic on a cattle boat. In Africa he met a man named Texas Jack, who ran a Wild West Circus. Rogers got a job as a trick roper, billed as The Cherokee Kid. (Rogers was part Cherokee.) He stayed with Texas Jack's show for 14 months. Then suddenly the urge to travel hit him again. This time Will headed for Australia where he landed a job touring with the Wirth Brother's Circus. When he had earned enough money, Rogers decided to go to San Francisco and then finally home.

But Rogers didn't stay in Oklahoma very long—only long enough to get acquainted with his future wife, Betty Blake. He soon went to St. Louis and joined up with another touring wild west show that took him to New York City. Once he got to New York, Will determined to try his roping hand in vaudeville.

Will Rogers works out with a lariat. Rogers was an expert horseman and trick roper.

Will was an expert trick roper, and he worked up an act that was successful with the sophisticated vaudeville audiences. Then one night at Keith's Union Square, for the first time Will began to talk with his audience, explaining what he was going to do. The audience roared with laughter at his explanation. Will Rogers walked off stage furious. He said he would never go back on again. But the manager of the theatre and other performers convinced him that he *should* talk in his act; he was a natural comedian. Will had been amusing people he knew for years with his funny stories and humorous sayings. All he had to do to amuse an audience was to be himself. So Will became a cowboy comedian.

In 1915 Florenz Ziegfeld saw Rogers' act and hired the cowboy for the Midnight Frolic. This was a late-night show at Ziegfeld's fashionable rooftop nightclub. Rogers did rope tricks and talked. He talked about everything, but was most successful when he talked about current events. Will's wife was the one first to suggest that he talk about the news since, as she put it, he spent so much time reading it. So Will Rogers talked about the President. He talked about Democrats. He talked about Republicans. And he talked about Congress, which he said was funnier all year long than anything else he ever read about. His comments were funny, but they were also sincere, frank, and down-to-earth.

Cowboy Will Rogers on stage with a group of Indian maidens (Follies girls).

Rogers worked in the Midnight Frolic for the run of the show. Then Ziegfeld decided he wanted this cowboy and his humorous, home-spun wisdom for the Follies. Rogers' personality made him as successful in the Follies as he had been in the Frolic. In time Rogers even became a close friend of Florenz Ziegfeld, a man who had few close friends.

Will Rogers' humor was unique for his time. He didn't tell jokes just to make people laugh but also to make them think about what he said. Yet he wanted to tell the truth about people without hurting them, and he could usually make even the butts of his jokes laugh at themselves. One night in 1918 President Woodrow Wilson and his wife were in the Follies audience. Wilson was at that time under attack from the press for taking too many trips abroad. But when Rogers took a poke at the President, he made Wilson roar with laughter: "I see by the papers that our President's going to Europe again. I don't believe he wants to go, but the old gal's got her clothes made and I guess he'll just have to tag along."

Rogers was also a hard worker. Some comedians used the same jokes and the same acts over and over again. Will Rogers changed his jokes every night so that the many people who came to see a show more than once would be amused by something different.

And Will Rogers did not seem affected by his great success. Many people said that offstage he was just as sincere as he seemed onstage. He earned a lot of money as a performer, yet he and his family lived modestly. Rogers gave away much of his money to charities and friends because he felt they needed it more than he did.

Will Rogers was killed in 1935 when an airplane he was copiloting crashed in Alaska. People all over the United States were shocked. They wept for him and they mourned his death. They built memorials to him. He had been a performer they admired and a person they had loved.

Eddie Cantor

Eddie Cantor

(1892-1964)

Eddie Cantor landed his first job on Broadway with a juggling act called Bedini and Arthur. He was hired just to press costumes, run for sandwiches, and do general backstage work. But one day he was told to come on stage at a signal and hand Bedini a plate. Eddie decided that this was his big chance to be discovered as an entertainer. So he worked for hours on his makeup and costume and decided to take his time giving Bedini the plate. When the signal came, Eddie went on stage, looked at Bedini, looked at Arthur, looked at the audience with his big saucer eyes, and then finally gave Bedini the plate and walked off. He got a laugh. And from that time on Eddie Cantor was billed on the program.

Cantor was born in New York City's Lower East Side, and Isadore "Izzy" Iskowitch was his real name. He was raised by his grandmother after both of his parents died when he was quite young. She made a living for the two of them by selling notions and running an employment agency for servant girls. She worked hard, but they were very poor.

Eddie later admitted that he didn't have any money to pay to see shows when he was a small boy. So he used to sneak into theatres after the first intermission. (The ushers never checked small boys for their ticket stubs.) Eddie would wait around a theatre lobby, eating something, during the intermission. Then he would walk in for the second half of a show — just as if he had been there all the time.

When he was just into his teens, Eddie gave his first stage performance at Miner's Theatre, a variety house in the Bowery. On Friday nights, anybody could perform. The best act got a prize. Eddie Cantor did impersonations of stage personalities. He didn't win the prize his first Friday night, but at least he wasn't booed off the stage. So the next Friday he went back, and this time he won.

As a result of his performance at Miner's Theatre, he joined a burlesque company that toured small towns in the East. But Cantor's impersonations were not very successful because the small-town audiences did not know who he was impersonating. Even worse, just four weeks after he had started with it, the whole show folded in Shenandoah, Pennsylvania.

Eddie Cantor performing in blackface. Because of the influence of the Negro minstrel show, many comedians of the time wore blackface in their acts.

When 17-year-old Eddie got back to New York, he found work as a singing waiter in a Coney Island cafe. Then, from Coney Island, Cantor went to Hammerstein's Theatre with Bedini and Arthur. After his plate-handing bit, he was given the opportunity to do a small act by himself. Bedini and Arthur broke so many plates on the main stage that the stage hands needed a lot of time to clean them up. So Eddie Cantor performed in front of the main curtain to give them enough time to clean up the stage. This also gave Cantor the chance to prove himself as an entertainer. Soon he got his first big break, a spot in a show called *Kid Kabaret*. The $75 a week he earned was enough so that he could marry his childhood sweetheart, Ida. Eddie and Ida had one of the happiest show business marriages ever known.

Cantor's second big break came in 1916 when Florenz Ziegfeld hired him for the Midnight Frolic, Ziegfeld's rooftop nightclub. Eddie graduated to the Follies in 1917. But when the 1919 show ended, Cantor was out of a job. Ziegfeld wasn't even speaking to Eddie because he had taken part in an actors' strike. However, Eddie's career continued to skyrocket. In 1924 Ziegfeld lured him back to do two musicals. (Ziggy had gotten over his anger.) The shows, *Kid Boots* and *Whoopee*, turned out to be two of Cantor's greatest successes.

Eddie Cantor was not a great singer or dancer. But he had so much energy and joy that audiences loved him. He used that energy and his good sense of timing to capture their attention as soon as he made an entrance. In *Kid Boots* he came on stage jiggling and bouncing up and down. Then he told the audience, "I've just bought a second-hand watch, and this is the only way I can keep it going." People laughed, and people loved him.

Besides being an excellent performer, Eddie Cantor was an outstanding humanitarian. He gave his time and support to a number of charities. He did benefit shows for the Red Cross, for orphans, for old people, for blind people, refugees, the March of Dimes, and many other charity organizations and disadvantaged groups. Eddie Cantor was always willing to help people as well as entertain them.

The Pull Ahead Books

AMERICA'S FIRST LADIES
  1789 to 1865
AMERICA'S FIRST LADIES
  1865 to the Present Day
DARING SEA CAPTAINS
DOERS AND DREAMERS
FAMOUS CHESS PLAYERS
FAMOUS CRIMEFIGHTERS
FAMOUS SPIES
GREAT AMERICAN NATURALISTS
INDIAN CHIEFS
PIRATES AND BUCCANEERS
POLITICAL CARTOONISTS
PRESIDENTIAL LOSERS
SINGERS OF THE BLUES
STARS OF THE ZIEGFELD FOLLIES
WESTERN LAWMEN
WESTERN OUTLAWS

We specialize in publishing quality books for young people. For a complete list please write

LERNER PUBLICATIONS COMPANY

241 First Avenue North, Minneapolis, Minnesota 55401